108 Rudimental Street Beats, Rolloffs, & Parade-Song Parts

In the Style of "Traditional" Drum & Bugle Corps

by John S. Pratt

ISBN 978-1-4234-6430-3

HAL•LEONARD®
CORPORATION

7777 W. BLUEMOUND RD. P.O. BOX 13819 MILWAUKEE, WI 53213

In Australia Contact:
Hal Leonard Australia Pty. Ltd.
4 Lentara Court
Cheltenham, Victoria, 3192 Australia
Email: ausadmin@halleonard.com.au

Visit Hal Leonard Online at
www.halleonard.com

CONTENTS

About the CD:

Solos 2–45, 47–95, and 97–99 are played twice on the CD. All other solos are played as written.

Performers from the Field Music Section
of the U.S. Military Academy Band:
(recorded in 1968)

John S. Pratt—Snare Drum
Willard Putman—Tenor Drum
Keith Trombly—Bass Drum
Glen Gould—Trumpet

PREFACE

After World War I, many of the American Legion Drum and Bugle Corps dressed in military garb, most of them wearing tin helmets, shirts and ties, dress coats with midriff leather belts that were joined by a leather cross-belt coming down from the left shoulder, and black or brown boots that met their trousers below the knees. Later on, some corps changed their uniform style to what the West Point cadets wore on the parade field, but as the old saying goes, "Variety is the spice of life." This could also be said in regard to the instrumentation of the drum section of the Drum and Bugle Corps, for it was not too long before an instrument called the tenor drum, which was merely a snare drum without snares, would join the ranks of snare drums, bass drums, and cymbals.

The tenor drums, with a tonal quality very much like the tom-toms of the Native Americans, produced a sound that blended with the snare drums and bass drums, providing a greater distribution of rhythmic voices, especially where contrapuntal playing was concerned, and proved to be readily adaptable to the rudimental figures of the snare drums. In any event, the 128 rudimental street beats, rolloffs, and parade-song parts in this book have been written in an attempt to introduce the various ways in which the tenor and bass drum can be utilized in filling out a particular drumming cadence and to demonstrate that the by-play between snares, tenors, and bass drums can be of a most interesting rhythmic nature. I trust that the beats in this book will stimulate a more active interest in "Traditional" parade drumming and will provide the drum sections of parade or drilling units with a varied repertoire of performance material. The various street beats, rolloffs, and parade-song parts should also be helpful as exercises in sight reading for drummers in intermediate stages of development.

It is important to know that the style of "Traditional" Drum and Bugle Corps ends with the material written for this book. There have been so many additions of instruments to competition corps nowadays that they could never consider themselves as "Traditional" Drum and Bugle Corps. For example, in competition corps marching at contests, a pit band on the sidelines has now become a standard addition for most corps shows, with orchestral instruments such as xylophones, marimbas, timpani, bells, and chimes backing up the corps marching on the field. Finally, one of the highlights of all Drum and Bugle Corps contests used to be a Color Presentation featuring the American flag. Unfortunately, we have witnessed a steady decline in Color Presentations in recent years to the point where they are rarely seen, if at all. It would seem to me, that alone would provide the strongest dividing line between a "Traditional" Drum and Bugle Corps and the other corps who are not interested in maintaining tradition. We should keep in mind that no stars, other than the original 13, were ever added to the American colonial flag.

John S. Pratt
Hawthorne, N.J.

FOREWORD

The year of 2009 marks the fiftieth anniversary of the very first published works by now legendary percussion composer John S. Pratt. To celebrate this mark, Hal Leonard Corporation is very pleased to re-issue *128 Rudimental Street Beats, Rolloffs, and Parade-Song Parts*, along with several forthcoming works by Mr. Pratt. I am very excited that Hal Leonard is making these materials, with new prefaces and corrected music, available once again.

John (Jack) S. Pratt, U.S. Army retired, is one of America's greatest rudimentalists, percussion composers, and finest gentlemen. Now internationally known for his compositions, teaching, and historic performances, Jack was an instructor of the U. S. Military Academy Band "Hellcats" drum line at West Point. Jack was also an instructor of the Hawthorne Caballeros drum and bugle corps drum line, which won four DCA World Championships and three American Legion National Championships under his direction. Jack founded the International Association of Traditional Drummers (I.A.T.D.) in 2004, which recognizes rudimental drumming excellence, and promotes and preserves the "Traditional" drumming art form. He was inducted into the World Drum Corps Hall of Fame, American Patriots Rudimental Drummers Club Hall of Fame, the Percussive Arts Society Hall of Fame, and the New Jersey Drum and Bugle Corps Hall of Fame. Jack deserves honor and recognition for his life-long commitment to rudimental drumming excellence and for his enthusiasm in passing on the art of "Traditional" Rudimental Drumming. I anticipate that *128 Rudimental Street Beats, Rolloffs, and Parade-Song Parts* will reinvigorate your study of "Traditional" Rudimental Drumming and provide material for your drum line, marching bands, percussionists, library, and/or general drumming pleasure.

Ben Hans
January 2009

100 RUDIMENTAL STREET BEATS

F - Right Flam

(F) - Left Flam

* Asterisks under tenor drum notes
indicate that these notes are also
played by the bass drum.

By JOHN S. PRATT

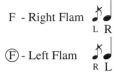

Track 1

Snare Drum

1

Tenor Drum

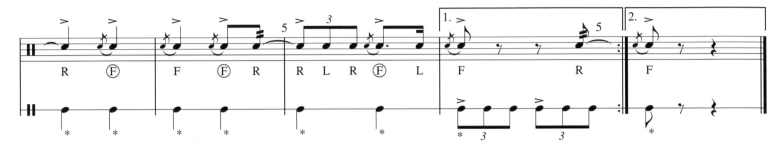

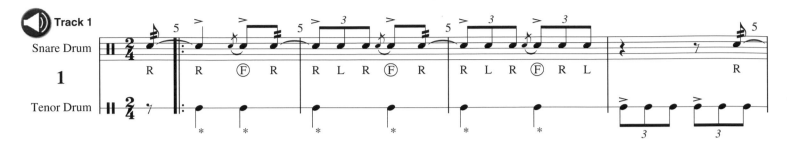

Track 2
(0:00)
(0:18)

2

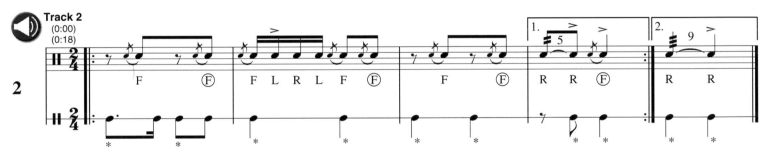

Track 2
(0:20)
(0:39)

3

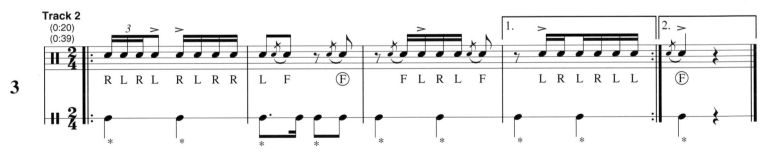

Track 3

4

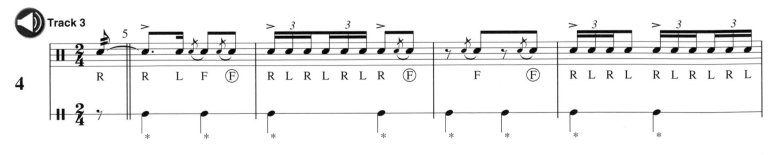

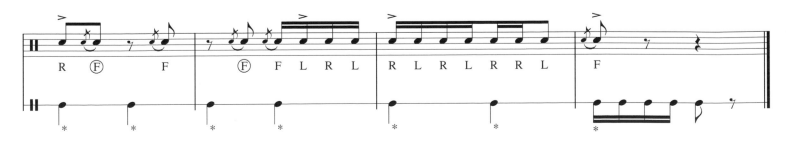

6

8

16

18

22

26

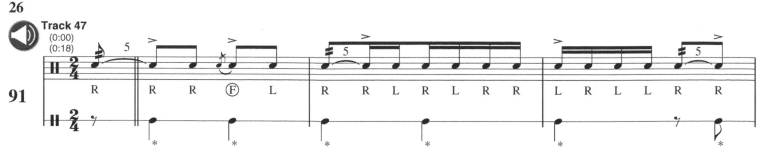

91

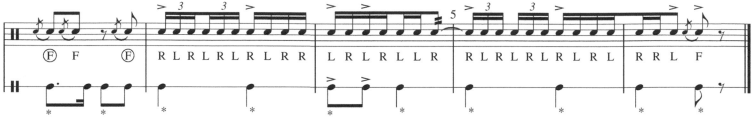

92

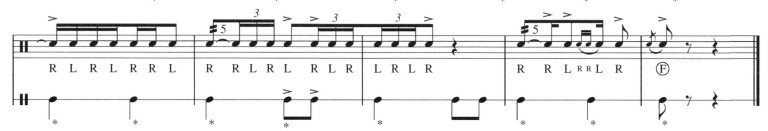

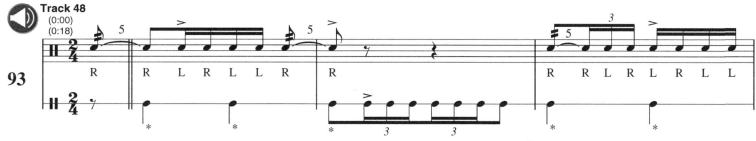

93

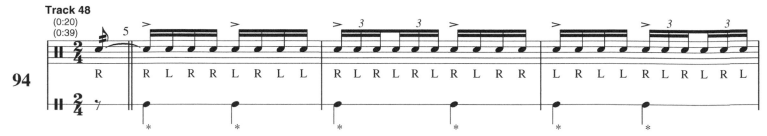

94

Track 49

95

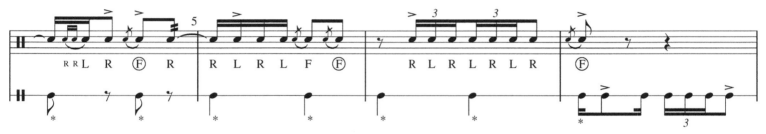

Track 50

96

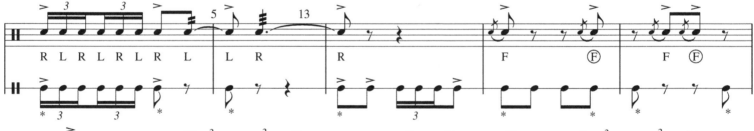

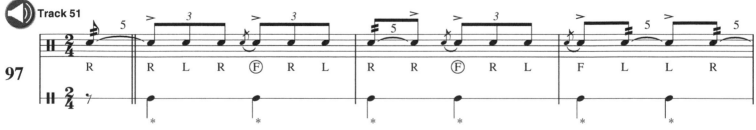

Track 51

97

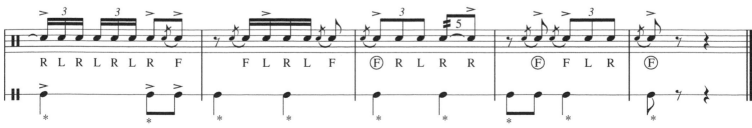

28

20 RUDIMENTAL ROLLOFFS

30

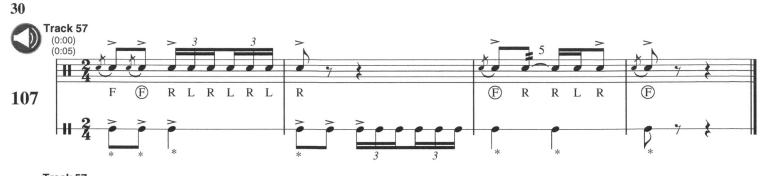

Track 57
(0:00)
(0:05)

107

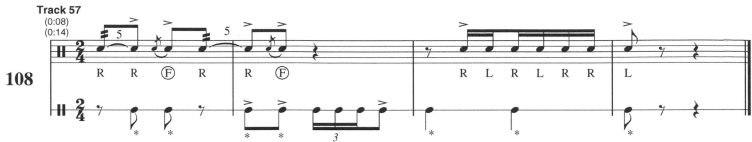

Track 57
(0:08)
(0:14)

108

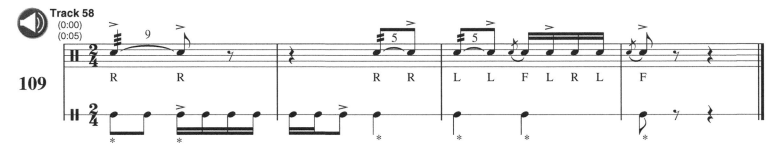

Track 58
(0:00)
(0:05)

109

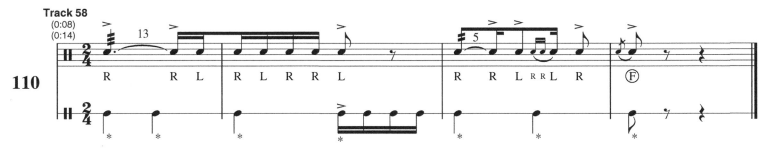

Track 58
(0:08)
(0:14)

110

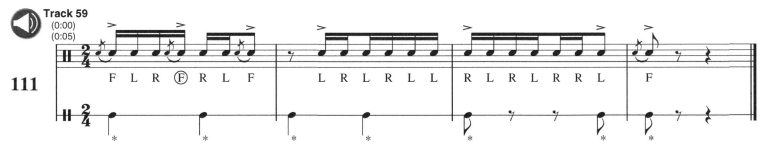

Track 59
(0:00)
(0:05)

111

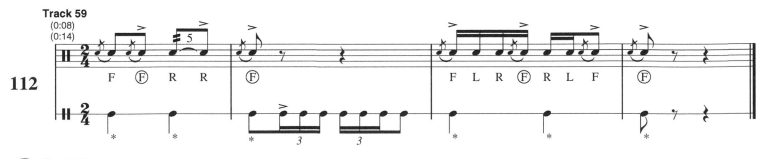

Track 59
(0:08)
(0:14)

112

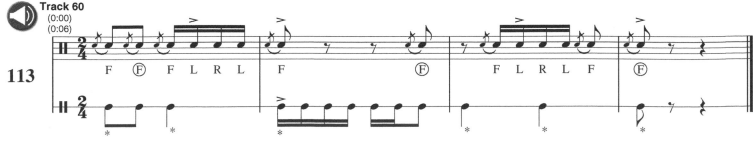

Track 60
(0:00)
(0:06)

113

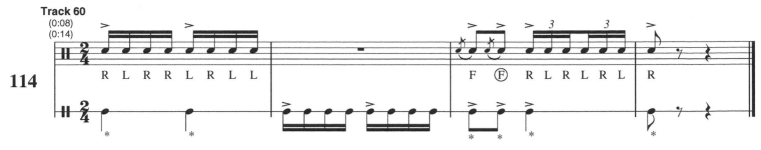

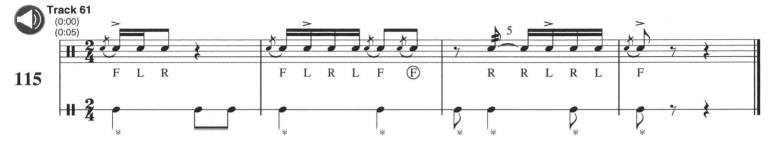

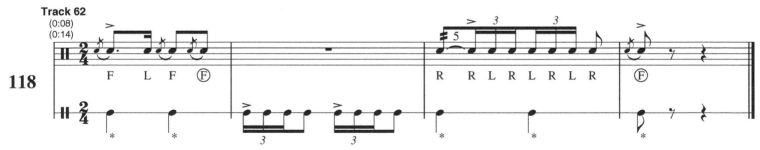

8 RUDIMENTAL PARADE-SONG PARTS

The following rudimental parade-song parts are examples of how the drum rudiments may be used to complement the phrasing and also provide a strong background for a particular tune or melody. Modern drum and bugle corps used this type of drum score or similar ones with great success after World War II into the 1970s.

This drum beat can be played to the tune of "Great Day."

121

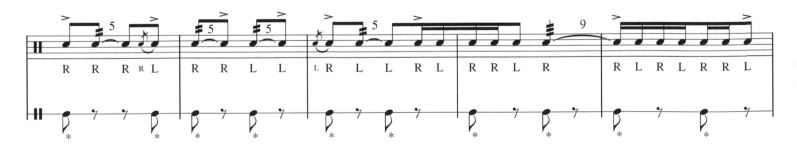

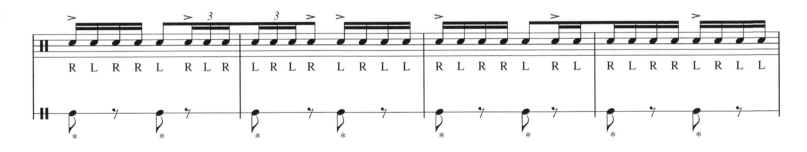

This drum beat can be played to the tune of "This Is My Country."

Cadence = 126-132

122

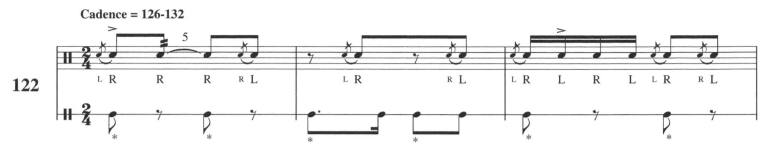
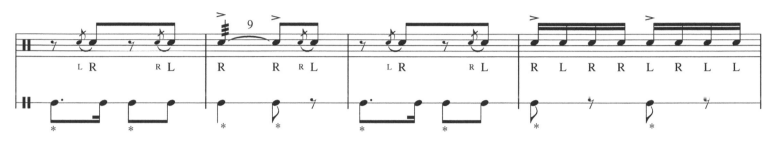
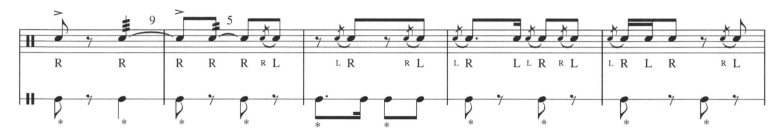

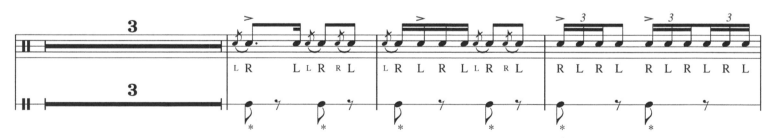
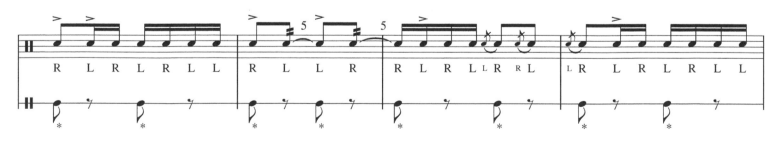

This drum beat can be played to the tune of "Waiting for the Robert E. Lee."

Cadence = 126-132

Track 64

123

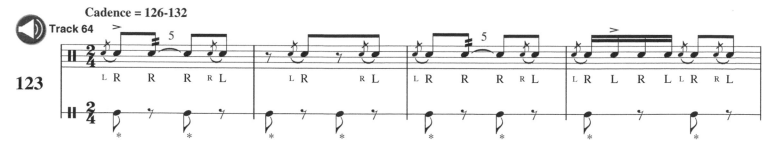

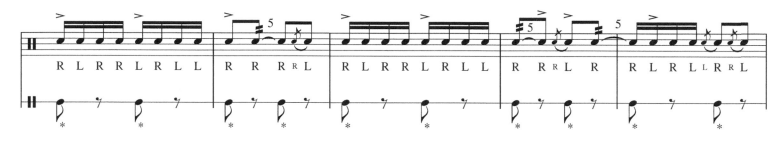

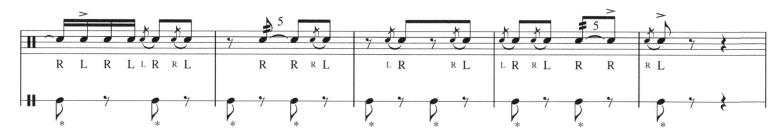

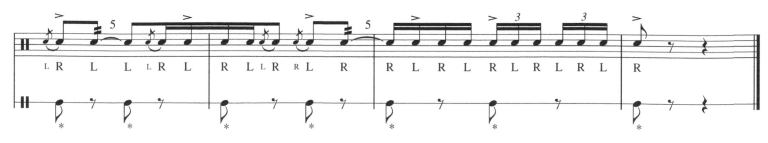

This drum beat can be played to the tune of "California, Here I Come."

Cadence = 126-132

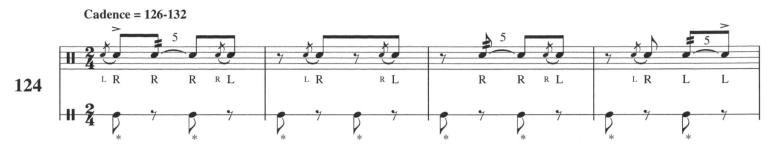

124

This drum beat can be played to the tune of "Good News."

Cadence = 126-132

125

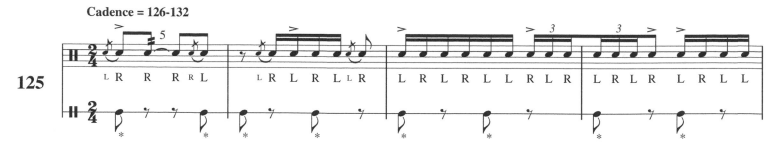
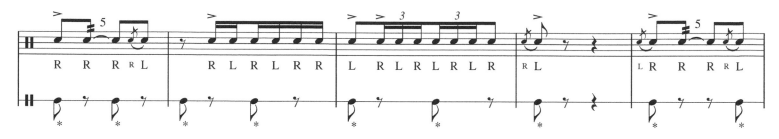
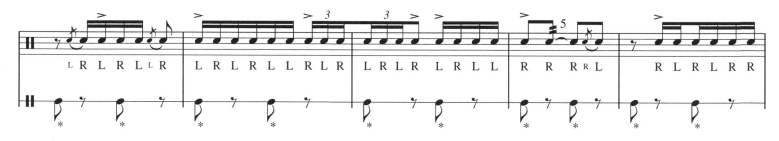
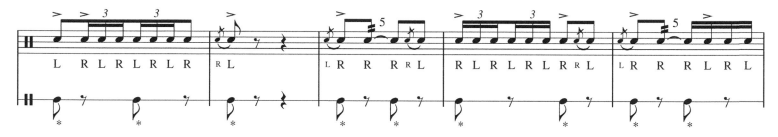
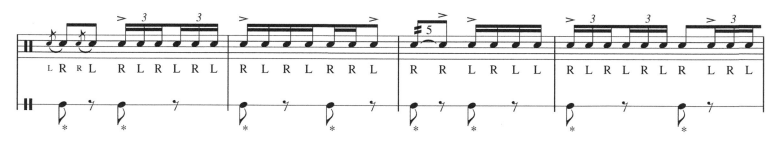
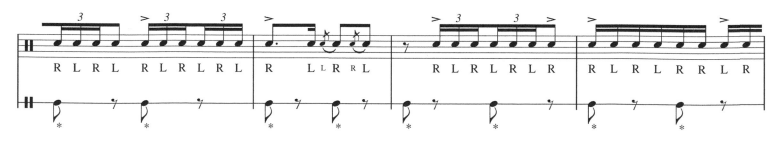
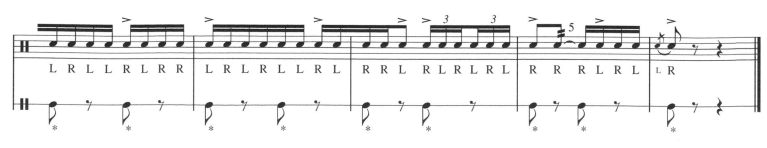

This drum beat can be played to the tune of "Oklahoma."

Cadence = 126-132

126

This drum beat can be played to the tune of "Yankee Doodle Boy."

Cadence = 126-132

Track 65

127

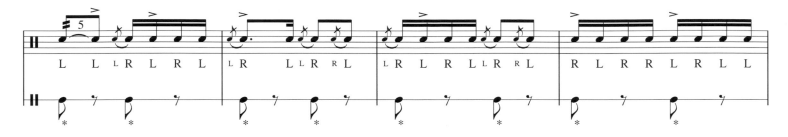

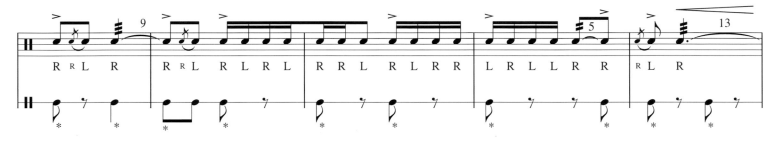

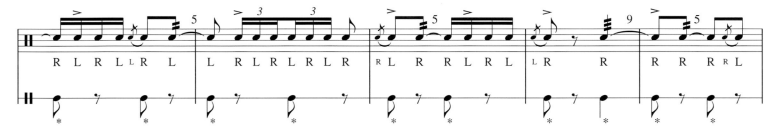

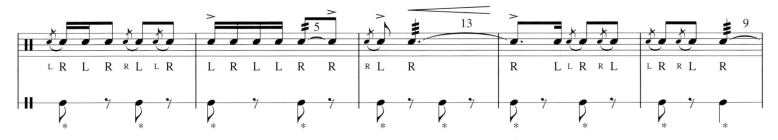

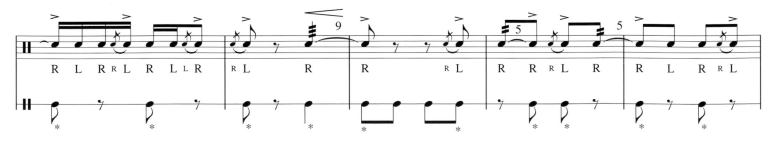

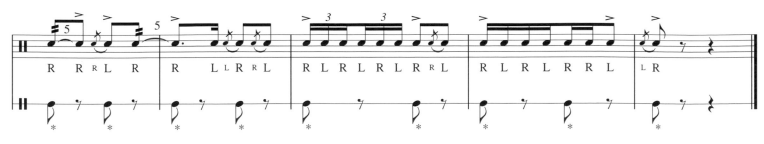

This drum beat can be played to the tune of "Alabamy Bound."

** Reverse flamacue

FOCUS ON FUNDAMENTALS

WITH HAL LEONARD SNARE DRUM BOOKS

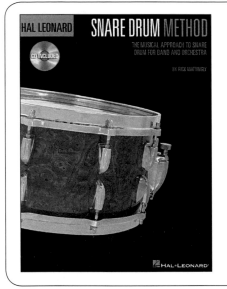

HAL LEONARD SNARE DRUM METHOD
The Musical Approach to Snare Drum for Band and Orchestra
by Rick Mattingly

Geared toward beginning band and orchestra students, this modern, musical approach to learning snare drum includes a play-along CD that features full concert band recordings of band arrangements and classic marches with complete drum parts that allow the beginning drummer to apply the book's lessons in a realistic way. This book/CD pack also includes: fun-to-play solos and etudes; duets that can be played with another drummer, a teacher, or with the play-along tracks on the CD; studies in 4/4, 2/4, 3/4, 6/8 and cut-time; roll studies that can be applied in both rudimental (double-stroke) and orchestral (buzz-stroke) style; the 40 Percussive Arts Society International Drum Rudiments (including modern drum corps rudiments); and much more!
06620059 Book/CD Pack $10.95

40 INTERMEDIATE SNARE DRUM SOLOS
by Ben Hans

This book provides the advancing percussionist with interesting solo material in all musical styles. It is designed as a lesson supplement, or as performance material for recitals and solo competitions. Includes: 40 intermediate snare drum solos presented in easy-to-read notation; a music glossary; Percussive Arts Society rudiment chart; suggested sticking, dynamics and articulation markings; and much more!
06620067 .... $7.95

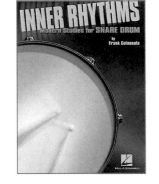

INNER RHYTHMS – MODERN STUDIES FOR SNARE DRUM
by Frank Colonnato

This intermediate to advanced-level book presents interesting and challenging etudes for snare drum based on the rhythms of contemporary music, including a variety of time signatures, shifting meters and a full range of dynamics. These studies will help improve reading skills as well as snare drum technique, and will provide insight to the rhythmic demands of modern music.
06620017 .... $7.95

MODERN SCHOOL FOR SNARE DRUM
by Morris Goldenberg

This book of 54 progressive solos and duets makes performing easier! Part 1 offers well-graded exercises to improve playing skills, and Part 2 covers all percussion instruments, helping percussion groups develop an ensemble feeling. Includes orchestral examples from Bartok, Bernstein, Rimsky-Korsakov, Stravinsky, Prokofiev, and more.
00347777 .... $12.95

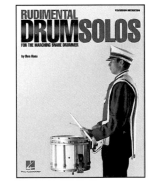

RUDIMENTAL DRUM SOLOS FOR THE MARCHING SNARE DRUMMER
by Ben Hans

Provides the advancing percussionist exciting solo material in the rudimental style. Meant as a study for developing the rudiments in a musical manner, it is designed as a progressive lesson supplement and as performance material for recitals, contests, and solo competitions. Includes: solos featuring N.A.R.D., P.A.S., and hybrid drum rudiments; warm-up exercises; suggested stickings, dynamics, and articulations; a music glossary; and more.
06620074 .... $12.95

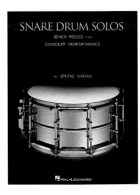

SNARE DRUM SOLOS
Seven Pieces for Concert Performance
by Sperie Karas

These solos provide excellent performance material for recitals and solo competition, and are perfect for use as lesson supplements. Seven solos include: The Fast Track • Hot News • Lay It Down • The Right Touch • Rollin' and Rockin' • Strollin' on Six • Waltz for Jazzers.
06620079 .... $5.95

FOR MORE INFORMATION, SEE YOUR LOCAL MUSIC DEALER, OR WRITE TO:

HAL•LEONARD®
CORPORATION
7777 W. BLUEMOUND RD. P.O. BOX 13819 MILWAUKEE, WI 53213

www.halleonard.com

Prices, contents and availability subject to change without notice.

0609